Alfred Leach

The Letter H

Past, Present, and Future

Alfred Leach

The Letter H
Past, Present, and Future

ISBN/EAN: 9783337158767

Printed in Europe, USA, Canada, Australia, Japan

Cover: Foto ©Thomas Meinert / pixelio.de

More available books at **www.hansebooks.com**

THE LETTER H

PAST, PRESENT, AND FUTURE

A Treatise:

WITH RULES FOR THE SILENT *H*, BASED ON MODERN USAGE;

AND NOTES ON *WH*.

By ALFRED LEACH.

A breath can make them. . . . . .
GOLDSMITH.

GRIFFITH & FARRAN

SUCCESSORS TO NEWBERY AND HARRIS,

WEST CORNER ST PAUL'S CHURCHYARD, LONDON

E. P. DUTTON & CO., NEW YORK

MDCCCLXXX.

PREFACE.

THE contradictory rules that are given for the employment of H's, and the confusion that reigns in our best Pronouncing Dictionaries, constitute an apology for the appearance of this publication. To promote an uniform pronunciation based on the sole authority of contemporary usage, is one of its purposes. To draw attention to the nature of the present English Aspirate, is another. To seek redress for the digraph WH, is a third. To render the subjects as interesting to the general reader as the matter would allow, has been the great desire of the writer.

It is with gratitude that I beg to express my thanks to the gentlemen whose kind courtesy I have acknowledged on page 56; and to Professor Bain, Professor Skeat, and His Eminence Cardinal Archbishop Manning, to whose kindness I am indebted for assistance in the

form of valuable comments and advice. I beg
also to thank the Rev. W. H. Bleaden, curate
to the Bishop of Aberdeen and Orkney; and
John Davidson, Esq., Memb. Arts Club, London, for the friendly help they have given me.

A. L.

YUDU VILLA, THORNTON HEATH,
October 1880.

CONTENTS.

8 CONTENTS.

PREAMBLE.

A WRITER in a high-class American periodical *
recently expressed his surprise that no English
orthoepist or phonologist had made the subject
of Aspirates and their misuse one of examina-
tion, or of more than a mere passing remark.
True it is that in works where dissertations
on single vowels occupy pages, and paragraph
after paragraph teems with analyses of individual consonants, "poor letter H" is often
summed up in a sentence. And yet it is no
exaggeration to say that, socially, H is of
English letters the most important, and that a
systematic trifling with half the vowels and
consonants of the alphabet would not be
visited with such severe social reprobation
as is the omission or misplacement of an H.

The fraternity of English Grammarians have,
it might seem, conspired to withhold from us
the means of propitiating this demon Aspirate,
which a study of its attributes would afford.
Mr Punch, that excellent censor of British

* ENGLISH IN ENGLAND. By R. Grant White.   In the
March number of the *Atlantic Monthly Magazine*, 1880.

manners and customs, has been the chief (not to say only) constant attendant to the English H-evil; but the fleam of his satire—an instrument as powerful, and often more effective, than the Thor-hammer of the *Times*—has scarified the abusers of H, without removing much of the abuse.

The American writer alluded to above enters, with the characteristic daring of his countrymen, upon the treacherous grounds of statistical definition, and states that, in England, "of the forty millions of people, there cannot be more than two millions who are capable of a healthy, well-breathed H." He is treading in safer paths when he says :

There is a gradation, too, in the misuse of this letter. It is silent when it should be heard, but it is also added, or rather prefixed, to words in which it has no place. Now the latter fault is the sign and token of a much lower condition in life than the former.

He appears, however, to write in ignorance of the customs of many good speakers, and of the opinions of several English orthoepists, when he adds: "Only Englishmen of the very uppermost class and finest breeding say *h*ome and *h*otel; all others, '*ome* and '*otel.*" Further on, he says :

H, in speech, is an unmistakable mark of class distinction in England, as every observant person soon discovers. I remarked upon this to an English gentleman, an officer, who replied—'It's the greatest blessing in the world ; a sure protection against cads. You meet a fellow who is well-dressed, behaves himself decently enough, and yet you don't know exactly what to make of him; but get him talking, and if he trips upon his H's that settles the question. He's a chap you'd better be shy of.'

This writer's friend, the "English gentleman," is spokesman to a large class. As the chemist employs a compound of sulphur in order to decide by the reaction whether a substance belongs to the group of higher or of baser metals, so does society apply the H-test to unknown individuals, and group them according to their comportment under the ordeal. There can be no doubt that a tendency of the age is to over-rate the value of H as a critical test for refinement and culture.

Although instances of well-educated persons who aspirate their vowels wrongly are extremely rare, the partial or even complete omission of Aspirates is far from being an absolute criterion of ignorance or vulgarity. The writer has in his mind's eye a very excellent and scholarly gentleman, one of the high dignitaries of an order of professional speakers, who, by strange anomaly, is a sad non-conformist in the matter of H's. But— need one add ?—such deviations from rule are as rare in their occurrence as the credentials of learning and social rank must be exceptional that can obtain forgiveness for them in society; and any man about to choose for himself an eccentricity is not advised to select the uncommon one of erudite H-dropping.

The prevalent disregard shewn for the rules of aspiration by classes of moderately well-educated persons, may be traced to several causes. Young children do not manifest any fine appreciation of the difference between aspirated and unaspirated vowels, and readily acquire a tendency to neglect or misuse the H, so that, unless correctness of aspiration be made a canon of the nursery, these infantile transgressions are liable to develop into deeply rooted habit. At a great many middle and lower class schools H-dropping is fostered rather than destroyed; the boys, with all that ingenuous ruffianism that preceding generations so admired in the youth of Britain, discountenance *forcibly* anything like "affectation," and, if H-droppers be in the majority, render it expedient in the youthful orthoepist to sink his singularity of right in deference to the dominant powers of wrong. A correct pronunciation, when once discarded, is not easily regained—lost H's have a knack of turning up in wrong places, when they return at all. Schoolmasters are not always models of correctness, and a staff of H-dropping ushers is not likely to impress school-boys with a regard for the Aspirate. Nor is it only in educational institutes of an inferior order that neglect, and even intolerance, is shewn respecting the full and proper employment of H. The writer could point out more than one of our very best English schools where (within the last three decades) school-boy tyranny forbade that WH should be pronounced other than W; and "wip" and "weel" were the only recognized renderings of *whip* and *wheel.* The uncertainty attending the words in which the H should be silent, is doubtless also partly accountable for its indiscriminate employment.

Before inquiring into the history and nature of Aspirates and their symbols, it may not be uninteresting to take a cursory glance at the extraordinary misuse of H in the Metropolis. The "Cockney Problem" has long been a puzzle to all except superficial observers. One may speculate reasonably as to the probable cause of the Londoner dropping his H's when he ought to aspirate them; but why he persists in placing H's where they should not be, seems beyond the powers of reason to explain. The problem is not solved by saying that an H is prefixed in order to emphasize certain words in a sentence, unless at the same time it can be shown that the speaker is consistent in his manner of using it, and that he is not in the habit of putting H's before unemphatic words. This cannot be shown; whereas the reverse can be demonstrated. To take an extreme instance: the Cockney will wrongly aspirate even the little words of a metrical composition, which are neither im-, portant nor emphatic ; and this, moreover, when they are out of accent. In his colloquial speech, *Horkney hoysters*, *'amshire 'am*, and *'am and heggs*, are expressions he employs with a provoking impartiality for the proper and improper use of the H. Stress may have something to do with some of these anomalous uses of the Aspirate, but to what extent is very far from clear. Eggs are perhaps brought more to the fore by becoming *heggs*, and an H may add to the importance of oysters ; but by what occult method of ratiocination he vindicates his invidious distinction between the rightful claims of ham and the imaginary requirements of eggs must be left for those to explain who can. Various are the suggestions that have been made relative to this phenomenon of misplaced H's; and if assurance could constitute authority, or the outcome of guess-work be accepted as proof, many of the suggestions would be amply supported in their demands for universal regard and acceptance. Some have believed that aspiration of the vowels is dictated solely by a desire to improve their sounds ; others, that a tendency exists to aspirate every initial vowel (as in Hindostanee), but that exceptions are made wherever they favour fluency and adapt them-selves to ease of articulation. Some, again, say that a pervert method of aspirating had an early origin and has undergone a process of gradual development until the acme of depravity has been reached by the present generation. Or, to add to the list, one might submit that the employment of H's is subjected merely to the purposeless choice of individual speakers ; but that the habit of class-conformity, so inherent in Londoners, is the cause of the prevalent misuse of the Aspirate by certain portions of the com-munity. Each of these theories, however, is found, when tested, to be of very restricted application, or little other than hypothesis : the Emphatic Theory must be acknowledged to be weak ; that of Euphony jars with fact ; the

Theory of Adaptation is observed to disagree
with practice ; the Theory of Development has
no historical basis ; and that of Elective Aspiration is arbitrary, and would compel us to re-
nounce our speculations concerning a subject it
cannot satisfactorily explain.

One may ask and attempt to answer the question : Why has H-dropping been made the butt
of ridicule in the present century only ? Perhaps
one reason is that, formerly, the words in which
silent H's were expected to occur were slightly
more numerous and even less clearly agreed upon
than they are to-day. But a better explanation
may be that the H of the past was too distinctly
audible to be omitted or inserted unconsciously;
whereas the modern dropper of H's is ludicrous
in that he remains in blissful ignorance of his
errors. It is certain that had H-dropping struck
our forefathers as risible, or ridiculous, or had it
been regarded as the trade-mark of vulgarity, it
would have been made capital of by the satirists
of the period. During the latter half of the last,
and beginning of the present century, however,
the strong English H gave place to the delicate
vowel-aspirate, with all the anarchial confusion
of laws, use, license and abuse which accompanies it to-day; and the H became appreciable to refined ears only.

ORIGIN AND DESCENT.

MANY attempts have been made to discover the origin of Chirography—the art of writing. Looking back, far back, over the populous plains of Time, the eye of Research seems to have perceived four or five germinal spots whence sprang the primitive parents of all known Alphabets.

The early "untutored savage," who chanced to be provided with an idea he deemed worth recording for the benefit of his fellows, had recourse to what artistic talent he possessed, and roughly expressed his idea in the language of permanent sign. Two circumstances will have conspired to lighten his labours : the first, that a habit of making known his ideas by means of an outward code of signals, will perhaps, have been even more familiar to him than that of expressing them through the medium of speech ; the second, that the burden of his thoughts will not have been heavy with deep or intricate abstractions difficult to express. His rude inscriptions gave rise, in course of time, to the word-painting of China, the picture-writing

B

of Mexico, and to the hieroglyphs of Egypt. Our business is with the last.

The truncated sparrows and *cavo rilievo* crocodiles, constituting the sculptured eloquence of the ancient Egyptians, were found too cumbersome for general purposes ; so they ultimately became converted into two varieties of a running hand—the *hieratic* and the *demotic* characters. These were Alphabets. One of the characters—a figure suggestive of a circle, of dissolute habits, with a stroke through it— seems to have been the founder of the House of H. The latest edition of the *Encyclopædia Britannica*, however, gives ⌒⊔ as being the earliest representative of the H's. The character first alluded to had this form, ⊝. The Phœnicians, who derived their Alphabet from Egypt, appear to have been desirous of "squaring the circle," for in their hands this became ⧗ , or ⧖. The Greek letter was at first ⊟ ; but later on it changed its appearance, becoming H. As such it figures in the Sigean inscription of the sixth century, B.C. Had the Greeks imported their letters directly from Egypt, one might have supposed *theta* (⊖, or θ), and not *eta* (H), to have been the immediate descendant of the Egyptian symbol given above. The Samaritan

ℶ, the Chaldean and square Hebrew ח (*cheth* or *heth*), bear marks of a common origin with the Phœnician H, although their general appearance has been brought into conformity with the general appearance of the alphabets to which they respectively belong.

The astonishing changes of shape seen in early letters, are also accounted for by the nature of the processes by which they were usually formed, as when a scribe would endeavour to write quickly with a metal style on a soft tablet; or an explanation of them may be found in the alterations that will, from time to time, have suggested themselves to the fancy of the cali- graphist. Extreme credulity and extreme scepti- cism are, as a rule, found blended in the natures of those people who refuse to believe that a chain can have existed if any of its links happen to be lost; and lest any such persons find the differences of form in the above H's to be an obstacle to a belief in their descent from a com- mon ancestor, some specimens of evolution quite as wonderful are selected from more modern typography, and given below—

ℌ 𝕳 ℋ ℍ Ⱶ ℋ

Tradition asserts that the Greeks received

their alphabet from the Phœnician Cadmus (1493 B.C.). There is reason to believe that H had its formal representative among their oldest letters, although Pliny states it to have been introduced after the Trojan War. Mr H. N. Coleridge* says, with regard to the Greek :— "After H (or η) was appropriated to express the long E, the rough breathing was not indicated in writing at all till the time of Aristophanes of Byzantium, who divided the H, and made one-half of it (Ⱶ) the mark of the aspirate, and the other half of it (⊣) that of the *lene.* By degrees these marks became ⌣— and —⌣ ; and hence, in the cursive character ' and ' marking the vowels." These last signs (' and '), Professor Geddes humorously styles, "the ghosts of a vanished consonant."

" This practice of spiritualizing, or of sending letters aloft, that were supposed to have a turn for climbing, has always existed in languages (*Encyclop. Brit.*, 1842)." As examples we have the two dots and the line ⁻ that hover over some words, and may generally be recognised as being the shades of a departed *e.*

The Romans derived their alphabet from the

---

* *The Greek Classic Poets*, 1834.

Greeks; and the Roman characters are those now in general European use.

The claims of H to a high respectability are conclusively established by a genealogical review of its ancient lineage. It may be that

" Some storied urn, or animated bust "

may yet be the means of calling back the forms and " fleeting breath" of many of the unknown and rude forefathers of H, that are now lying in the great mysterious Asiatic burial ground.

DISTRIBUTION.

OUR attention may now advert to the phonetic significance and distribution of the symbols of which we have just considered the historical aspect.

The sounds represented by the earliest alphabetical characters can only be a subject for conjecture; the sounds of those we have had under consideration were probably very pronounced, ranging from that of a strongly guttural *kch*, to that of the jerked breath occurring in a short, emphatic, English "bah!"

We have seen that the Greek character was early mutilated; but the rough-breathing powers of the Greek H were transferred to the sign ' and we may conclude that the Greeks were at one time very partial to the *asper*, their writers finding it necessary to prefix a special sign, the *lene* ('), when vowels were *not* to be aspirated.

In Latin also the H was at first harsh; but later on indications occur of the decline and fall of the Roman H in the fact of Quintilian complaining of the h-dropping propensities of his contemporaries. In his time, Latin writers already affected great freedom even in the orthography of words containing an H ; its presence or absence in such words as *honestus*, *ahænus*, &c., being apparently viewed with considerable indifference. Cicero strongly censures its gratuitous introduction into words. The Romans are thus responsible for ancient (if not venerable) precedents in eclectic H-dropping.

The Sclav and Latin languages have treated the Aspirate with spare courtesy, having let it become the mere " shadow of a sound," or allowed the letter to dwindle into an altogether insignificant symbol. In Italian, "that soft bastard Latin," the H is practically a dead letter, and has left no legitimate offspring. The Tuscan dialect, however, has afforded a local habitation to all the banished H's of Italy ; and the saying, "*Lingua toscana in bocca romana*," may be held to be an indirect allusion to the dislike that the Italians bear to the Aspirate. In French, the H is never an Aspirate ; it merely *hardens* the vowels in certain words, *e.g.*, *haie*, *hameau*, *hieroglyphe*, &c., and its office is a sinecure in others. When it hardens a vowel, it forbids a *liaison* with the last consonant of the preceding word. But in Spain, letter H is

treated with systematic barbarity. Not only is
its presence disregarded, but, since the days of
the Almoravids (eleventh century), or even from
an earlier date, its rightful office as an Aspirate
has been usurped by letter J. Besides this, its
literal identity has been allowed to get con-
fusedly mixed up with that of the letter F ; so
that Latin words while undergoing the process
of acclimatization on Spanish soil have been
observed to exchange an H for an F, *e.g.*, Lat.,
facere = Sp., *hacer*, which is nevertheless pronounced " acer." A reverse permutation oc-
curred in the Sabine *fircus* (a buck) and the
Latin *hircus*.

The Slavonic tongues are weak or deficient
in H's. In Russian H has the value of N.

Turning to the Teutonic and Keltic stocks,
one notices a marked contrast in the fortunes
of H. In High German it has retained an
important and prominent position ; although,
generally speaking, it is less conspicuous in Low
German tongues. The simple Aspirate, and the
other and harsher varieties of H, were universally received into the Keltic languages ; the
Cymric branch shewing a slight preference for
the former, and the Gaelic for the more guttural
variety. Prof. Geddes remarks : " The Gaelic

alphabet contains a letter to which, apart from a partial parallel in Greek, I am not aware of an exact parallel in any tongue. It begins no words, heads no vocabulary in the dictionary, and yet is found everywhere diffused over a Gaelic page." Something partly similar appears to exist in Sanscrit, a highly aspirated language with seemingly no purely initial H. Max Müller* and most other writers give $\overline{\text{ᕬ}}$ as being the Sanskrit H, whereas some affirm it more properly to represent *gh*.

Arabic and other Shemitic languages abound with Aspirates ; in the former, at least, they do stalwart service. Throughout that large group of languages which resist systematic classification, and are chiefly known through the works of Tylor, Lubbock, and others, or still more recently through the agency of the missionaries, —*e.g.*, the languages of North America and of Polynesia—Aspirates are copiously distributed. The Maoris are wont to substitute an H for several of the European speech-sounds, against which their vocal organs rebel.

In English, the omission of H's that ought to be heard, is peculiar to England, and especially

* *The Sacred Books of the East* (1879). The Upanishads, page lv.

marked in London and the Southern counties.
The Lowland Scotch are free from the defect;
and the people of the Highland districts and the
North run to the opposite extreme, and give to
their H's a strong guttural sound. The Irish
and Welsh are also free from it. Men of English parentage and American birth, New Eng-
landers, Virginians, &c., are correct in their use
of the Aspirate (vide *Atlantic Monthly*, No.
269). That the Americans are without this
H-trait, may be accounted a result of the pre-
dominance of North British and Irish immi-
grants.

His Eminence Cardinal Manning, when
favouring the writer with some valuable notes
on the subject of Aspirates, gave, as his opinion,
that the dropping of H's in England cannot be
explained by foreign influences. The Aspirate
is put on and put off in certain counties—as in
Middlesex and Gloucestershire—with long local
traditions; and he believes that, like the Greek
digamma, it refuses all submission to criticism.

HISTORY OF THE ENGLISH H.

THERE is something startling in the announcement that were William Shakespeare to hear one of his plays read by a good speaker of our own day, it would be less intelligible to him than if spoken in the Somersetshire dialect. So great is the change in English pronunciation. This fact prepares us for the discovery that great alterations have taken place in the significance of individual letters ; and that the phonetic value of letter H has changed also. -

Dr Johnson, in 1755, wrote : "Grammarians of the last age directed that *an* should be used before H, whence it appears that the English anciently aspirated less."

"The great Doctor uttered many hasty things."—
Thackeray.

Dr Johnson's suppressed premiss is negatived by his own *protégé*, Goldsmith, in whose writings *an* occurs before every variety of H ; a fact which shows that *an* and the Aspirate were not generally considered to be incompatibles. That their juxtaposition does not of itself offend the modern ear, may be proven by uttering the words "*than have*" and "*they have*," in which the Aspirate is heard to follow the *n* and the vowel-sound with equal grace and fluency. There are, moreover, many reasons for entertaining an opinion directly opposed to that expressed by the great lexicographer; and for believing the powers of the English H to have been steadily on the decline since the days of primitive English. In all Aryan languages, H has a tendency to mollify and decay; and its powers are always found to be most strongly marked in Germanic tongues that are in nearest historical relation with their common Teutonic ancestor.

Inductively, one is led to believe that the English Aspirate is less strong than formerly. This belief will acquire support from the following argument :—

It will be remembered that prior to the introduction of terminal rhymes, the laws of Prosody were based upon principles slightly different from those of to-day; our ancestors, preferring an identity of consonant-sounds to an assonance of vowels, required that syllables to rhyme should *begin* with the same letter—the system being known as ALLITERATION. If we bear in mind how much must have depended on the distinctness and strength of the alliterative rhymes of early verse, where the metrical management and rhythmical cadence were far from being irreproachable, we shall readily concede that the bard will have selected for his use the strongest and most distinct rhymes that the language could supply. "Rhymes to the eye," as they are called, would have been utterly useless, from the fact of poetry being then composed for oral rendering, and the hearers generally ignorant of spelling. It is, therefore, agreeable to reason to conclude that all sounds employed in alliterative rhyming were distinctly audible, strong, and emphatic. Now, on looking over alliterative verses of the seventh to thirteenth centuries, one cannot fail to be struck by the frequent occurrence of rhymed H's: their proportion being, in many poems, in excess of that of any other letter. Modern poets, it is true, have not unfrequently pressed H into service as an alliterative rhyme, but in so doing they have afforded ample proof of the inefficiency of the modern English Aspirate, when acting in that capacity. One of the best specimens of

modern alliterative H-rhymes is that in one of
Moore's American poems :—

"And I said, ' If there's peace to be found in the world,
A *h*eart that is *h*umble might *h*ope for it *h*ere.' "

But the alliteration is scarcely appreciable, unless the rendering be accompanied by undue
aspiratory efforts. Whenever we hear a run of
words rhyming alliteratively in H, it is highly
probable that only half the pleasure we experi-
ence is conveyed to us by ear, and that the other
half is of a subjective nature, and arises from
our *knowing* the letter H to enter into the formation of the words, and the alliteration would be
almost lost to us were we ignorant of their
orthography. Hence, it is rather from an associa-
tion of ideas, than from an effect produced on
the organs of hearing, that we derive the
pleasure ; and the modern H, indicating as it
does merely a like modification in the phonation of the several vowels to which it is prefixed,
cannot be regarded as having a *distinct sound*
of its own, nor, consequently, as constituting a
perfect alliterative rhyme. Do not the mute
H's of the following words give results nearly as
satisfactory as the H's in the above quotation?—

The *h*eir that is *h*onest will *h*onour the *h*our !

Considering, then, the faintness and the nature of the Aspirate of to-day, and its insufficiency for purposes of alliteration, we seem at liberty to conclude that the Anglo-Saxon and Early English H, so much affected of the early poets, was stronger than our own, and had, in all probability, retained much of the pristine power of its Teutonic harshness.

That the sound of the Anglo-Saxon H bore a resemblance to that of an unvocalized *y* (see page 37), is made manifest by the free interchange of *h* and *y* in ancient MSS. The substitution of surds for sonants, and *vice versâ*, is common to the early stages of the development of all orthographical codes.

Mr Ellis, whose researches have thrown great light on these matters, gives as his opinion—

In Anglosaxon, a final h *was equal to the* ch *of l*och, *or German d*ach. *In the thirteenth century the sound of* H *seems to have been very uncertain, and in the fourteenth it was lost in those words before which a vowel was elided. In the sixteenth it was pronounced or not, differently from the present custom.**

There exists a belief—perhaps on no very firm foundation—that the Normans could not, or would not, aspirate their H's; and the idea

* EARLY ENGLISH PRONUNCIATION, *with especial reference to Shakespeare and Chaucer.* By Alex. J. Ellis, F.R.S.

gains some support in the period of decadence
of the strong English H having commenced
subsequently to the Norman invasion. It is,
however, not easy to understand how these
Norsemen should have learned to entirely aban-
don the use of H in consequence of a century
and a half's residence in Neustria. Salesbury,
a Welsh linguist, exhumed by Mr Ellis, implies moreover that, as late as the sixteenth
century, the French still aspirated at least *some*
of their H's, and Littré, in his admirable dictionary, declares the Norman Aspirate to be in
a state of good preservation (" *très-nettement con-
servé* ") in our own day. The old Norse H had
been, according to Rask, Grimm, and Ellis, a
vigorous and thriving aspirate ; Rapp gives it as
having been equal to *kh*. But presuming that,
prior to the Invasion, the Normans had become
droppers of H's, would enable one to account
for the unsettled state of the English H in the
thirteenth century, when English reappeared
as a national speech (1258). Also, according to
this latter view, a habit of not aspirating would
have been greatly in vogue for a time, and for a
Saxon to have dropped his H's would have been
equivalent to an announcement of good breeding
and aristocratic acquaintances, or of his being

in the habit of frequenting the court and other haunts of the Norman nobility. But when the language of the vanquished began to overcome that of the conqueror, the Aspirate must have entered upon a new era, and H's again have prevailed in the land. Still the new H had not the vigour of the old one—the guttural of the Anglo-Saxon. In the fourteenth century, as mentioned by Mr Ellis, its employment was subject to various rules ; and this will have probably been the period during which the first mute H's received public recognition, being tolerated as a sort of compromise or concession made to an aristocracy little partial to H's. Throughout the remaining centuries there have been rules of some sort governing—though very laxly—the employment of the Aspirate. But the powers of H were gradually, surely, and steadily waning, until, at length, its strong guttural sound finally and completely evanesced towards the latter half of last century.

Presuming that the reader consents to recognise the antique origin, the unbroken line of descent, and the rough, sturdy ancestry of our English H, it may be interesting to notice that in 1847 appeared the second edition of a critical work on the English Language,* written in

* *Kritishes Lehrgebändes der englischen Sprache.* Leipzig.

German (by a fellow of Cambridge), purporting among other things to prove to the omniscient Teuton, that in England the aspiration of H's is altogether a modern invention, a fanciful outcome of recent orthoepical dogmatism ; and that by good speakers it is practically ignored. Concerning this writer, Mr Ellis says, "His principal argument is the retention of *an, mine, thiye,* &c., before words beginning with H, in the authorised version of 1611. The lists of words with mute H given by Palgrave, Salesbury, &c., were of course unknown to him. If, however, he had been aware of the loose manner in which H is inserted and omitted in Layamon, the 'Genesis and Exodus,' Prisoner's Prayer, and other writings of the thirteenth century, he would doubtless have considered his point established. In practice, I understand from a gentleman who conversed with him, he omitted the H altogether."

MODERN ASPIRATES.

THE English H has been variously classified, and still more variously and vaguely defined. Some phonologists have discovered in it the properties of a vowel; most have agreed to regard it as a consonant. Webster declared it to be "not strictly a vowel nor an articulation, but a letter *sui generis*"—a negative classification that may be accepted to-day. The letter has been termed the symbol of a guttural breathing, an evanescent breathing, a mere breathing, a strong breathing, a whisper, and "a propulsed aspiration" (*B. H. Smart*); and some affirm it to be "no sound at all."

The English H represents an action rather than a sound. When the action indicated accompanies the utterance of a vowel, a change is produced in the vowel-sound; hence, Bishop Wilkins (1668) called the H a "guttural vowel" —not, however, a particularly happy definition.

In stating H to be "a letter *sui generis*," Webster enounced a truth that many have seemed inclined to overlook. Consonants are distinct sounds that precede or follow other consonants and vowels; but the Aspirate becomes part of any vowel it accompanies. This may be otherwise expressed by saying, that in aspirating we emit a noiseless current of unvocalised breath that gradually vocalises itself into an aspirated vowel. The truth of the assertion may be tested by pronouncing an aspirated vowel, *e.g.*, "**ha,**" and observing that no change in position of the vocal organs occurs during the act. In uttering a syllable consisting of a consonant and a vowel, a change of position is requisite to the formation of each constituent element—for example, in the case of "**fa.**" Thus then, the H in well-spoken English does not represent a distinct and inde pendent sound ; but prescribes a breathing that modifies the vowel it accompanies. It is A SIGNAL TO ASPIRATE THE SUCCEEDING VOWEL.

This oneness of the vowel and its H is productive of a change in the natures of both. The *a* in "h*a*ll" is as different from that in "*a*ll," as is the Aspirate of "*h*all" from that of "*h*eel." It follows, therefore, that these Aspirates are equal in number to the vowel-sounds (said to be about seventeen), and that the letter H represents them all. For convenience sake,

one speaks of "the sound of an H," "to pronounce, or aspirate an H," and "to drop an
H ; " meaning respectively, *the sound of an
aspirated vowel, to aspirate,* and *to omit to
aspirate a vowel with an H before it.*

As already submitted, most H's may, now-a-
days, be said to be *soundless*, although not "Silent
H's ; " the latter might with more propriety be
termed functionless letters. To soundless H's
one exception distinctly occurs in English ; to
wit, the H that precedes the long *ū*, as in *hue,
huge, humor*, &c. This H—a phonetic link
between the ancient English H's and the modern
Aspirate—has a sound of its own, and may be
heard. Elevating the base of the tongue so as
to leave a narrow aperture between its centre
and the palate, we emit, with vocalized breath,
the sound *y* heard in *yew* ; with breath that is
not vocalized we produce the subdued, palatal
grating sound constituting the H of *hue.* Hence,
HŪ represents a vowel *preceded by an audible* H,
and not a vowel-sound that is aspirated. The
Arabic ح corresponds to the H of HŪ.

Other kinds and degrees of H are enumerated
by Mr Ellis, who gives a list of six. They vary
in power from that of the scarcely audible
aspiration that the Cockney introduces into

" park " (paahk), to that of the jerked breath
that *h'* represents in *bah'*. The breathings of the
different H's vary also in degree of intensity
according to the nature and strength of their
vowels ; being most pronounced in the case of
long and open vowels,—compare " *h*ard " and
" *h*it."

Some writers have described aspirated vowels
as being whispered vowels. The error of this
description is obvious to the most superficial
observer ; it would mean that aspirated vowels
are unvocalized. A man, moreover, need not
drop his H's though he holloa through a speaking trumpet.

Vocalized breath is that which carries with it a sound
produced by vibrations of the vocal chords. These
are situate in the larynx, and may be felt vibrating, by
placing the hand on the throat while they are in action.
" Krantzenstein and Kempelen have pointed out that the
conditions necessary for changing one and the same sound
into different vowels, are difference in the size of two parts
—the oral canal and the oral opening," (*vide* Kirkes' Physiology). Some consonants are produced by this kind of
breath, but with the concurrence also of certain movements of the lips, tongue, &c., and they are called *sonants*
or *voiced consonants :* Ex.—*l, n, r,* &c.

Unvocalized breath is that employed in whispering.
With the assistance of certain movements of the speech-
organs, unvocalized breath produces in ordinary speech a
class of consonants that are called *surds* or *breathed consonants :* Ex.—*f, s, t,* &c.

NOTE.—*T* is of the class called *momentary* or *explosive* consonants. They need the help of a vowel, or of a voiced consonant, in order to express themselves fully. This circumstance, together with the fact of vocalised breath entering into the formation of many consonants, will probably account for the common notion that *no* consonant can be uttered without a *vowel* accompaniment. The independence of the sibilant *s*, offers alone a sufficient refutation of the assumption. It is in Polynesia that savages are found who cannot put two consonants together without a vowel between them.

Æsthetically considered, the modern English H is an important embellishment, and adds immensely to the strength and pleasing effect of speech. The Aspirate can render certain discordant sounds of our language half euphonious, breathing gently on a hard vowel, deepening its tone and swelling its volume. As an instance, take the pronoun *I* and the adjective *high;* and notice that the vowel-sound in the latter is by far the more pleasing, approaching almost that of the soft *ai* of the Italian. In oratory, a preponderance of aitch'd words in a passage allows of great energy of utterance without risk of it degenerating into an affected or bombastic tirade of "big-sounding" words.

H is an earnest letter. It is a noteworthy coincidence that a large portion of those words associated with strong and violent actions and emotions have the Aspirate: *hew*, *heave*, *hate*, *abhor*, &c., together with the ejaculations, *Ho !* *Ha! Hollo! Hurrah! Hang it!* (an exclamation used by Geo. Wither, born A.D. 1588), &c., are examples. In Elocution, the Aspirate lends itself to the expressing of propinquity, bringing the scene and the sound of the action within a more proximate compass. The union of H with most consonants results in the production of smooth sounds. The euphonic "sweetnesses" of Mr Swinburne's richly mellifluent verse, will be found, on analysis, to depend greatly on the two powers of TH and those of other digraphs of H. Writers on the subject of Natural Significance, or Specific Import of Articulate Sounds, who have mostly been adherents to the Epicurean or *Pooh-Pooh* theory, have in some instances limited the primary emotional significance of an Aspirate H to the denoting of a desire or craving. It may reasonably be asked, whether they have not identified a part with the whole, and whether every awakening of intense feeling does not find its natural expression in an aspirated vowel.

The manner in which the H is used by our best writers, shows they appreciated its vigour and stress-giving properties. In Shakespear, the H is most frequent in salient passages and epigrams. It plays a conspicuous part in the grand, deep anthem-eloquence of Dryden's full-toned lines ; and in the verses of Byron and other strong writers its powers are judiciously applied. A recognition of the honest vigour of aspirated words is conspicuous in an aphæresis perpetrated for histrionic purposes by Mr Henry Irving, who has informed the writer that he sometimes drops the H in "humbleness—"

"as in Shylock's speech to Antonio : *

> ' Shall I bend low, and in a bondsman's key,
> With 'bated breath and whisp'ring (h)umbleness,
> Say this . . . .'

where the idea is much better expressed by the omission of the Aspirate."

There are persons to whom the simple act of aspirating, will never have suggested the idea of difficulty ; but there are many others (who in their ordinary speech, put H before half the vowels that do not require it) who are totally at a loss when asked to aspirate a given vowel. They either aspirate unconsciously or not at all. If the reader has never attempted to reform a persistent H-dropper, by teaching him

* Merchant of Venice, Act i., Scene 3.

the value and nature of the Aspirate, he can form no adequate idea of the extreme difficulty of the task. Some people can learn everything but H's. "*Speak as though you were breathing on glass,*" is a practical precept often laid down for the benefit of young children; and is one deserving of the consideration of many of their elders; for, as a matter of fact, in pronouncing the words *hay, he, high, hoe,* before a mirror, one will observe that four successive breath-marks are thrown on the cold surface of the glass; whereas none will be seen if one drop the H's. In pronouncing the H of HŪ, the markings are scarcely discernable or altogether absent; the breath-stream having become diverted and attenuated by friction against the palate. In Aspirating *ha!* the breath-marks are very distinct; but still more so in the case of the jerked terminal *h'* of a quick, contemptuous *bah'!*

The above experiment is valuable as affording an insight into the phonation of the modern English Aspirate, and as a means by which the new convert from the H-dropping heresy may learn to avoid the opposite error of excessive zeal in the production of his H's. It is noticeable that the early aspirative labours of a converted H-dropper give birth to monstrosities.

He pronounces *hand*, *heart*, &c., as though the vowels were *preceded* by the *ch* of lo*ch*. This is a reversion to a former type of H's, but not the developed modern Aspirate. The physiological difference in the formation of aspirated and non-aspirated vowel-sounds appears to be, that, in aspirating, the oral passage is rendered more cavernous, and a greater volume of breath is emitted. This may be partly verified by uttering the Italian *ā* before the mirror. When the same vowel is aspirated (*ha*), the soft palate is seen to be slightly raised, while the tongue is depressed and slightly retracted, thereby causing an enlargement of the cavity through which the sound passes.

The H, in some positions, is not easily managed. In colloquial speech it is frequently left out of little words that are of minor importance to the sense. In a homely rendering of, "You saw how high (h)e held (h)is head," the occluded h's would be nearly lost. Such a pronunciation, though not one to be highly commended, finds its excuse in convenience, and can claim some degree of extenuation in a very antique origin, and of justification in extensive usage.

In the case of short, unaccented syllables of

a metrical composition, as in the following instance,

> " But Marmion said that ever near,
> A lady's voice was in *h*is ear,
> And that the priest *h*e could not *h*ear." . . .

and in this couplet—

> *H*e *h*eeds it not ; 'mid eddied *h*eaving foam
> *H*e *h*ears the echoes of *h*is island *h*ome,

difficulties are presented in the way of a regard for H's and for metre. Under all circumstances, to stop and stutter is inelegant, to repeat a word for the sake of giving it its dropped H, has a ludicrous effect ; and to attempt by a powerful effort to aspirate some particular vowel, will often result in a promiscuous scattering of H's. The only advice to the novice is : select difficult passages,* and practice them repeatedly —speak slowly and carefully. One must endeavour to aspirate with ease, letting the result be light, not forced, though distinct to the ear. Each person should use discretion, and suit the degree of aspiration to the power of his

* Persons who consider themselves experts in the art of aspirating might do well to procure " HARRY HAWKINS' H BOOK ; *showing how he learned to aspirate his H's,*" and put their aspirative faculties to a crucial test, by reading aloud the story of "The Hairy Ape." The little book cannot be too warmly recommended as a practical and amusing method of learning to aspirate.

voice. The degree suitable to some persons would require an effort on the part of others to imitate. The great thing necessary is once thoroughly to understand the nature of the process, and then to remember where to apply it. The performance will gradually become a result of reflex action and be gone through correctly but unconsciously.

H-dropping must be overcome, and the misuse of H avoided ; the world is intolerant of dissent from customs established ; and orthoepy, or correct pronunciation, is a cardinal virtue, although, in common with most other of the "orthos," it is endowed with chameleon-like faculties of change.

THE SILENT H.

IT has been seen that the letter H is a signal to aspirate. The term *mute, otiose* or SILENT H, implies that the signal means nothing, is useless, and is intended to be disregarded; that it is a false beacon, an orthographical encumbrance, and a trap for the unwary. Lumber of this sort is to be found in certain words, but in which ones, has always been a profound mystery from the fact of it having been so often explained; and information was unobtainable, by reason of a multiplicity of informants. Where the H is silent, has been difficult to determine; why the H is silent, cannot be determined at all. This much has long been divulged; it is silent in *hour, honour, honest, heir*, and most of their formatives; the rest is darkness—in the dictionaries. On no point of English pronunciation have authorities more notoriously disagreed than on that of words beginning with H; and if any one wishes to see the fathers of English Orthoepy at loggerheads, or the

Doctors of Modern English Pronunciation in a muddle, let him glance at the H section of their several dictionaries.

Be it, however, remembered that the work of the writer of pronouncing dictionaries is one of extreme difficulty, and that his short-comings are often of the most excusable kind to be met with in the whole field of literature. The etymologist has scientific fact to deal with ; the lexicographer is by tacit consent, and in virtue of that fiction of fictions " etymological conservation," allowed, to some extent, to jurisdict or appeal to precedent in matters of orthography ; but the professional orthoepist is expected to catch and register the passing sound of a nation's speech. There is no discretionary power attached to his office ; his duty is to discover who are representative speakers among his contemporaries, and—by a sort of arithmetical process—to determine what pronunciation is *prevalent* among them. Hence his entire task is one of appalling magnitude. But he has discovered a meretricious means of lightening his labours, which consists in referring to his predecessors in cases of extra uncertainty ; the result frequently being that he gives as modern an obsolete pronunciation. It is evi-

dent that several words in which the silent H is
concerned have undergone this treatment.

In the very good old times, ere spelling-
books had created " bad spellers," every writer
was, in a small way, a phonographer; that
is, he wrote words as he heard them pronounced. The system did not favour uniformity of spelling, but resulted in most words
being written in two or three different ways,
some in fifteen, or even twenty. Instead of
animadverting on the subject of these discre-
pancies, or attributing them to the undeter-
mined value and inadequate supply of alphabetical symbols, we may better serve our present
purpose by simply noticing that it was customary for early scribes to insert the letter H in
some words wherein it is now generally supposed
to have been silent. We see at once that the
facts of the case militate against this modern
belief in ancient silent H's. For, if the majority of these early penmen, whose minds were
neither in an appreciable degree biassed by
precedent, nor haunted by the forms of orthographical bogies, habitually inserted an H, it is
evident that the letter was intended to have a
phonetic significance, and had very probably a
strong phonetic value. The same conclusions

have been arrived at by Mr Ellis, who sees no reason for believing that H was not audible in *honor*, *honest*, and *hour* in the time of Chaucer —say 1400. Collateral evidence in support of Mr Ellis's views is to be found in the fact of the doubtful words occurring in alliterative verses of an early date ; and of their occurring in such a manner as to allow of the supposition of their H's being implicated in the alliterations as, what are termed by Professor Skeat, " rime-letters."

In the age of Chaucer (and, in diminishing degrees, down to our own day), it was customary to drop the H's of short, unaccented syllables in poetry, provided that these were not placed in a position immediately succeeding a metrical pause. But, as far as the writer is aware, the sixteenth century is the earliest that has furnished a record of any words having been habitually written with H's and pronounced without them. Palsgrave, in 1530, gave *honest*, *honour*, *habundance*, and *habitation* as having each an otiose H. Salesbury (1547), in his Welsh Dictionary, says that H is held silent in " French and Englysh, in such wordes as be derived out of Latyne, as these : *honest*, *habitation*, *humble*, *habit*, *honeste*, *honoure*, *exhibition*,

and *prohibition;"* whereas he aspirates it in
*h*umour.   Gill (1621) adds *hour* and *hyssop* as
having a mute H ; and aspirates in *h*erb, *h*eir,
and *h*umbleness.   Jones (1701) makes it mute
in *swine-herd, Heber, Hebrew, hecatomb, hedge,
Hellen, herb, hermit,* and some others.   Smart
(1836) reduced the whole list of words with a
silent H to *heir, honest, honour, hostler, hour,
humble,* and *humour;* and modern usage consents to a still greater reduction.

The suppression of H's has been observed to
have been chiefly exercised in words coming to
us from the Latin, through the French language.
It seems that Salesbury, quoted above, regarded
this, or something like it, as having been a rule.
But we find records of some words of neither
French nor Latin origin having also had silent
H's assigned to them; and we have the still
more important fact that the Franco-latin
words in which the H is aspirated are greatly
in excess of those in which it ever was silent
—the latter really constituting a very insignificant minority.   In the third line of *The Vision
of William,*

In *h*abite as an *h*ermit·un*h*oly of workës,

we have convincing proof that Langland (1332-
1400 ?) had no regard for the etymology of his

Aspirates. Certainly, French words of Latin
origin have constantly taken the aspirate when
their etymology was in the least obscure.
Thus, *hearse* (which most people do not know
is French, and still less do they think it represents the Latin [acc.], *hirpicem**) has always
retained its Aspirate. Moreover, it were one
thing to be able to prove that a certain pronunciation would be etymologically correct,
and another to show that the pronunciation of
a language is corrected by etymology. We are,
in fact, at liberty to regard the English silent
H, as being practically devoid of active etymological sponsors.

Taken collectively, these different data very
strongly suggest the idea of silent H's having
been, if not born of, at least very assiduously
fostered, and promoted with almost paternal
solicitude, by the judgment or fancy of theo-
retically-inclined orthoepists. If, on the other
hand, the early orthoepists were really honest
in their pretensions to chronicle the actual pronunciation of their day, the result of their
endeavours still remains open to the objection of
inaccuracy, by reason of the special difficulty
they will have experienced in recognizing a

* See Skeat's ETYMOLOGICAL DICTIONARY of the ENGLISH
LANGUAGE. *Oxford University Press*, 1880.

standard to go by. Nothing can, now-a-days, screen them from a suspicion of having exercised their powers of imagination equally with those of observation; nor can their partial disagreements exonerate them from the charge of a traditionary collusion in cases of extra perplexity. If asked, with what weight this same charge might be brought to bear on our more recent compilers of " modern pronouncing dictionaries," the writer of the present treatise would, under the plea of *coram non judice*, take refuge from the onus of pronouncing an invidious decision. But if asked why the comparatively modern dictionaries quoted on the opposite sheet, are, in some instances, so flagrantly at variance with the best modern usage with regard to pronunciation, he would unhesitatingly reply that they are so chiefly out of deference to the opinions of the gentleman who wrote the first complete pronouncing dictionary and lived over a hundred years ago.

If it be granted that of yore, orthoepists based their decisions with regard to the silent H on no other authority than that of their own assertions, or on dogmatic, or even spurious etymology, it flows as a corollary that these ancient law-givers can claim no allegiance from modern speakers. And again, if modern compilers of

DICTIONARY CONCORDANCES.

" H" prescribes the Aspirate ; " v ' indicates that the vowel is not to be aspirated.
The pronunciation recommended in this work is shown in the first column.

	Wk.	J.	O.	N.	Wor.	S.	R.	C.	D.	B.
HEIR .. ⎫ HOUR .. ⎪ HONEST. ⎬ HONOR . ⎪ and all their ⎭ formatives *except*	v	v	v	v	v	v	v	v	v	v	v
honorarium *and*	v			v			H		H	v	
honorary.	v	v		v		v	v	v	Hor v	v	
HERB . . .-	H	v	v	v	v	v	H	v	H	Hor v	H
herbaceous .	H	H	v	v	H	v	H	H	H	H	
herbage ..	H	v		v	Hor v	Hor v	H	H	H	Hor v	
herbal ...	H	H		v	H	H ⸴		H	H	H	
herbalist ..	H	H	.	v				H	H	H	
herbivorous .	H			v				H	H	H	
herborisation .	H,			v			H	H	H	H	
HOSPITAL.	H	v		H	H	H	H	H	H	Hor v	H
hospitalier .	H			H				H	H	H	
hospitable..	H	H		H		H	H	H	H	H	
HOSPICE ..	H			H			H		Hor v	H	
HOTEL ..	H			H	H		H	H	H	H	H

DICTIONARY CONCORDANCE S—*Continued.*

	Wk.	J.	O.	N.	Wor.	S.	R.	C.	D.	B.
HOSTEL ..	H	H	H	H	H		H	H	H	
hostelry ..	H	H	H	H	H			H	H	
Hostler ..		v	v	v	v	v	v	H	Hor v	Hor v
(*ostler*) ...	v									
hosteler ..	H				H					
HUMOR ..	H	{Smart proposed that this word, meaning moisture, fluids, &c., should be aspirated.}								
humoral ..	H	v		H	v	Hor v	H	H	v	v
HUMOUR .	Hor v	v	v	H		Hor v	v	H	Hor v	v
humourism .	Hor v			H	'	v	Hor v			
Humourist .	Hor v	v		H		v	v	H	Hor v	v
humourous .	Hor v	v		H		v	v	H		v
humoursome .	Hor v	v		H		v	v	H		
HUMBLE .	H	v	v	v	Hor v	Hor v	H	H	· or v	Hor v
HUMILITY	H	H		v			H		H	

A blank generally indicates that no distinct opinion is expressed in the work consulted.

KEY TO REFERENCES.

Wk. { Critical Pronouncing Dictionary. By John Walker. Glasgow: Blackie & Son. 1847.

J. { Dictionary of the English Language. By Samuel Johnson. 4th Edition. 1786.

O. { Comprehensive English Dictionary. By John Ogilvie, LL.D. London: Blackie & Son. 1874.

N. { Pronouncing Dictionary of the English Language. By P. Austin Nuttall, LL.D. London : Geo. Routledge & Sons. 1873.

Wor. { Critical Pronouncing Dictionary. By Joseph E. Worcester. London: Geo. Routledge & Sons. 1875.

S. { Etymological and Pronouncing Dictionary. By Rev. Jas. Stormonth. London: Wm. Blackwood & Sons. 1879.

R. { Webster's Improved Pronouncing Dictionary. By Chas. Robson. London: Ward, Lock & Tyler. *No date*—recent.

C. { Dictionary of the English Language. By Arnold J. Cooley. London and Edbro'; W. & R. Chambers. *No date*—recent edition.

D.—Chambers' Etymological Dictionary. By Jas. Donald, F.R.G.S. 1878.

B.—Bell's Standard Elocutionist. London : Wm. Mullan & Son. 1879, "pronouncing dictionaries," being the direct descendants of the ancient orthoepists, assume the right of hereditary legislation, and persist in their attempts to govern our modern pronunciation by the worthless traditions of their predecessors, the yoke of their archaical jurisdiction must be thrown off altogether. We may therefore approach the question of "What words now have silent H's?" entirely free from the bias of traditionary lore, and from the pressure of antiquarian and etymological considerations.

When preparing to obtain a firm basis upon which to found and sustain a plea for the recognition of a standard pronunciation founded on contemporary usage, the writer solicited the advice of Professor Bain, whose friendly assistance was partly conveyed in the following :—

"Where usage conflicts, we must first decide who are to be received as authorities. It seems to me that the stage is better than any other, and the habits of great actors might be referred to. The cultivated society of the metropolis ought to furnish a guide, but we can hardly fix upon a person representing them."

Acting according to the spirit of this advice, the writer has consulted the USAGE OF CULTIVATED SOCIETY as represented by a number of gentlemen whose various qualifications eminently fit them to fulfil the conditions laid down by Dr Bain.* The result of the inquiry, and of personal and attentive observation, furnishes the following rules :—

Rule I. **H is silent in Heir, Honest, Honor, Hour, and in their formatives, inclusive of honorarium** (15) **and honorary** (18).

The figures represent the number of persons (among those consulted) who adhere to the particulars of these rules.

Rule II. **In Humour and its formatives** (be they verbs, substantives, or adjectives) **the H may be either silent** (10), **or not** (9).

In Humor (meaning fluid, moisture, &c.) **and its formatives, the H is sounded.**

Rule III. **H is Aspirated in all other words in which it occurs.** These include the following and all their formatives—Herb (17); Hotel

* The following gentlemen kindly furnished the writer with an account of their habitual pronunciation of words in which the silent H is implicated :—Mr Matthew Arnold ; Mr Samuel Brandram ; Mr Robert Browning ; Rev. Derwent Coleridge ; The Very Rev. the Dean of Chichester ; Right Hon. W. E. Forster ; His Grace the Duke of Richmond and Gordon ; Professor Huxley ; Mr Henry Irving ; Sir Wilfrid Lawson ; His Eminence Cardinal Manning ; Sir James Paget ; Mr F. E. Sandys (Public Orator of Cambridge); Right Hon. Lord Selborne ; Right Hon. Lord Sherbrooke ; Rev. C. H. Spurgeon ; Very Rev. Dean Stanley ; Mr Edmond Yates ; and a distinguished member of the present Ministry (1880).

(16); Hospital (17); Humble (18); Humility (19), &c., &c.

NOTES. It is difficult to find a reason why an exception should be made in favour of *honorarium* and *honorary;* and, unless the H of these words can offer a better plea for entering into the pronunciation than can the H's of the other formatives of Honor, we may—after the style of Lucian in his trial of the letter T—move for its expulsion. The rejection of an anomaly is a valuable improvement of which judgment approves, and which a love of regularity will vindicate and maintain. Uniformity presents so many advantages, that small concessions of opinion will be willingly made in order to secure it.

With regard to *Hostler*, there is a balance of opinion —(8) being in favour of the Aspirate, and (11) against it. The pronunciation of the word should be made depend on the spelling.

In 1775, Perry waged war with Kendrick concerning the H of *Humour*, and threw down the gauntlet in favour of a y-sound. Subsequently, Enfield entered the lists on the side of Kendrick; while Walker, Sheridan, and a host of others, ranged themselves on the side of Perry; and Smart at length proposed that the respective claims of H and Y should become matters for the optional decision of a perplexed public. Hence the phonetic rendering of the word in most modern dictionaries is indifferently " yū′mur" or " hū′mur." Webster's verdict was curt and concise : " The pronunciation " yumur " is odiously vulgar ! " His words lose their edge in our day, for the " odious " practice prevails with a great number of good speakers. The present writer, if permitted to advance an opinion, would say that to his mind to drop the H " is a custom more honour'd in the breach than the observance ; " and that they secede in very good company who aspirate.

The H of *Humble* has of recent years been reinstated

in public favour by the late Mr Charles Dickens, whose
" Uriah Heep" remains a warning to evil-doers and
h-droppers. It would be a boon to all speakers of
English if a series of "Uriahs" could contrive to elimi-
nate every otiose H from the language.

H's that occur in the body of words, as in
fore*h*ead, ex*h*ibit, &c., are weaker than initial
H's; but a regard for them marks a refined
speaker. The h of "exhibition" may be considered lost, so also the h in the "ham" of
names—*e.g.*, Bucking(h)am, Bal(h)am, &c. Long
words, especially of a classic origin, often pay
dearly for suddenly acquired popularity; and
when any extraordinary event with which they
are nominally connected puts them accidentally
into the mouths of the people, they generally,
in becoming household words, are clipped of
much of their early dignity.

In parenthesis, a word about the indefinite
article. One very excellent grammar says :—

Many of the best writers, as Macaulay, use *an* before
H (not silent) when the accent is on the second syllable :
" *an* historical parallel."

Some words beginning with a vowel are pronounced
as if they began with a consonantal *y :* ewe, eunuch,
eulogy, European, useful, &c. Before such words some
writers use *an.**

A journalistic acquaintance lately informed

* A HIGHER ENGLISH GRAMMAR. By Alex. Bain, LL.D.,
Professor of Logic in the University of Aberdeen.

the writer that the use of *an* before *u* (when = *y*) is a feature of English journalism, the Scotch being more addicted to *a*. The former method is more correct to the eye; the latter to the ear: uniformity favours the former. The employment of *an* before H-out-of-accent (*e.g.*, hypothesis, harmonium, hiatus, horizon) is a nicety, and arises from a fastidious application of the law of Euphonic Adaptation.

Reverting for the last time to the history of the silent H, it is almost necessary to mention that an ingenious American writer (to whom we have already referred) was recently engaged disseminating opinions at variance with those adduced in this work. In a cleverly-written article, he says :—

I venture the conjecture, which, however, is somewhat more than a conjecture, that the suppression of H was once very widely diffused throughout England among all speakers, including the best, during which time—a very long one—the function of H was to throw a stress on the syllable which it ushered in, as it is in the Spanish word *hijos*.

He further suggests that vulgar h-dropping of to-day may be a survival of a former accepted method of pronunciation. *Se non è vero, è ben trovato*, and this recognition of the emphasizing power of H is highly commendable. But it cannot be conceded that the old English H was

normally passive, and only roused into phonic
activity on occasions of emphatic emergency;
nor can it be allowed that the Spanish com-
parison is a felicitous one, it being rather that
which an opponent might have adduced could
he have deemed it to have had any bearing
whatever on the point in question. This writer
ought to have borne in mind that the *h* of *hijos*
happens to be mute, whereas the *j* is an Aspirate.
There is nevertheless much valuable matter in
his article. It is moreover of service as an
example of error; its author having fallen into
a conclusion that lies open to those who allow
their attention and judgment to become ab-
sorbed in the frolics of H's in some of the old
MSS. He points out, for instance, that in the
"Lay of Havelok the Dane" (1280), the words
eye, earl, ever, &c., have H's; and he assumes
the spelling to have represented an allowable
pronunciation, neglecting, however, to take into
consideration that this Lay is among the worst
of examples, from the fact of its being essentially
a provincial production (Sir F. Madden believes
it to have hailed from Lincolnshire), and one in
which meaningless H's are uncommonly prevalent and letters are curiously placed. Although
ancient writers habitually endeavoured to write
a word as they spoke it, they did not resist the

temptation of occasionally adding an idle letter, or of employing one as an orthographical expedient. In modern German, H is made serve in the latter capacity; its duty being to lengthen the vowel that precedes it; *e.g.*, in the word *Bohn*, "give it an understanding but no tongue." The H prefixed to "eye" in Havelok, if not simply a scrivener's blunder, may be a result of metathesis or of commutation, or of the two acting simultaneously—Ormin (*circa* 1210) wrote the word "eʒhe." But, to refrain from speculative meanderings, one may refer to Mr Ellis, who mentions that in *Havelok* H is unnecessarily prefixed in holde (line 30), hete (146), het (653), hof (1976), &c., &c., and with no sort of uniformity; and, in giving the intended pronunciation, he affirms these H's to be meaningless as signs of aspiration.

The most that, with a due regard for fact and authority, can be conceded to the writer of the magazine article above referred to, is that H, being formerly a harsh sound, was not unfrequently omitted for the sake of fluency in the same manner as whole syllables are occasionally lopped off by careless speakers. This concession, by-the-bye, is not specified in his treatise.

DIGRAPHS.

WHEN two vowels are blended, the result is a diphthong; when two other letters unite, the result is usually called a DIGRAPH.

H may give trouble to some persons when speaking their mother tongue; as to the Briton, who should, and to the Frenchman, who must not aspirate; but the digraphs of H are universally admitted to be among the most serious difficulties that beset a man who is trying to acquire the pronunciation of a language not his own. The German *ich* is liable to dwindle into "ik" in the mouth of an Englishman, and into "ish" in that of a Frenchman; with Italians and some others it is unutterable. The modern Greek delta, and more especially $\chi\theta$, often undergo cacophonic metamorphoses when entrusted to the care of well-meaning philhellenists; a digraph of H enters into the phonetic composition of most of the shibboleths of Eastern tongues; and, in the estimation of many foreigners, the bugbear of our English pronunciation is spelt TH. In Britain, the *ch* of lo*ch* and Au*ch*termu*ch*ty remains the Caledonian pass-word.

The following are the more common digraphs of H :—

CH, GH, PH, SH, TH,
BH, DH, KH, LH, NH, RH, ZH,
WH.

The first five are perfect digraphs, a phonic union of parts is effected, and a new sound produced; thus, neither "hat," with the sound of c before it, nor "cat," with its vowel aspirated, will give the sound heard in "*ch*at," ∴ C+H is not =CH.

CH has three sounds:—*k*, (*ch*aos); *sh*, (ben*ch*); and a third, compound, tsh (*ch*ur*ch*).

GH is a digraph to perpetuate the memory of English orthographical anomalies.* It is used in writing seventy-five words, and in sixty-three of them its presence is ignored entirely; in nine it is equivalent to *ff*, and in three it represents a

* NOTE (*by Professor Skeat*).—There is 'a ridiculous notion that *u*, forsooth, *must* precede GH. Hence *thogh*, rightly pronounced with *o*, is actually spelt *though*. *Laghter*, rightly pronounced with *a* (as in Italian *a*), is spelt *laughter*. *Through* is quite correct : *ou* as in *soup*. Spellings like *caught, slaughter*, are not only mistakes for *caght, slaghter*, but the misspelling has affected the pronunciation. GH is a comic question altogether.

g. It signifies nothing in "hi*gh*," "Hu*gh*," &c.; and in "flight," "night," &c., it retains the same signification. In Old Saxon, and in Anglo-Saxon, "high" was written *hea, heag, hig, heah, heh, hih,* &c. A spirit of impartial justice instigated later writers to take in both the *g* and the *h*. Professor Meiklejohn (St. Andrews) mentions the opinion held by some, that the Normans would not pronounce gutturals, and disregarded the Saxon terminal *h*'s, wherefore the scribes attempted coercion by strengthening their Aspirates with a *g*. The result must have been a failure, since both the *h*'s and their g-prefixes became lost to the pronunciation of most words. The English words in which GH is an initial digraph are *ghastly, ghost,* and *gherkin;* in the two former the H is altogether adventitious. There exists a proneness to transpose the *h* and the *t* of *height*, (Saxon, *heath, hihth,* &c,), in consequence of which, and with a superfluous *d*, it becomes "heidth." This mispronunciation is recorded by Jones as early as 1701. The practice will arise from a natural tendency of the mind to bring into conformity the sounds of words that are associated in their meanings—leng*th*, dep*th*, bread*th*, wid*th* *ergo*: "heidth"!

PH has the sound of *f* (s*ph*ere). In Ste*ph*en and ne*ph*ew it stands for *v*.

SH is the French *j* (*j*oli), unvocalised. The Anglo-Saxons had not this digraph, but it appeared some centuries after the conquest, which suggests the possibility of its having been introduced by Norman influences. Some curious philologist may perhaps undertake to substantiate or demolish the theory that the Anglo-Saxons learnt to pronounce SH by attempting to utter the French *j*. Certain it is that the words *Je me jette à genoux* would become changed into "Sheh me shett ah sheenoo" by the average German of to-day. The substitution of SH for *ss* in the word *assume* produces an odd-sounding archaism, yet one that is occasionally met with in otherwise good speakers. According to Jones, "as*h*ume" was correct speech in the seventeenth century.

TH of *thin* and **TH** of *then* are elementary sounds represented now-a-days by two letters each. The former is produced by passing unvocalized breath through a narrow aperture left between the fore-part of the tongue and the edge of the upper teeth (the central incisors); the second by the same position of the speech-

organs, but with breath that is vocalized.*
Common errors are, to confound the TH of
bath, path, wreath, &c., with that of *bathe, paths,
wreathe,* &c.. The former are unvocalized, as
in *thin.*

Of the digraphs of the second row little need
be said. With one exception they are rarely
used. **BH, DH, KH,** and **ZH** are English renderings of the aspirated consonants of Asiatic
languages. **LH** is a legacy from the Anglo-
Saxon. **NH** is Portuguese. In **RH** the H is
excessively useless ; it is disregarded, and the R
remains unchanged. That man deserved to have
his name recorded who first invented the *h* of
"rhyme." He will have traced a technical con-
nection between *rime* and "rhythm ; " and will
have followed the latter to its Greek source
(ρυθμος). His next act, the insertion of *rime's*
apparently lost *h,* will have seemed to him one
only of mere reparative justice. His excellent
motives and his perspicacity might have met the
admiration of posterity, had not his etymology

---

* According to *Carpenter's Physiology,* to pronounce TH,
"the point of the tongue is applied to the back of the incisors,
or to the front of the palate." Such injunctions as these are
doubtless strictly followed out by foreigners learning English,
the unavoidable result naturally being that *thin* and *then* become approximately "sin" and "szen."

been so egregiously faulty, and the word *rime,*
a direct descendant of the Saxon *rim,* and as
independent of a Greek as of a Cherokee origin.
But the *h* he inserted is there still, and cannot
be cast off by any daring iconoclast without an
outcry being raised in its behalf by alarmed
traditionists: for our orthographical creed is
derived from our forefathers, impressed with
the accumulated evidences of their quaint blun-
ders, their venerable ignorance, and admirable
errors of judgment, all to be assiduously copied
by each of us their descendants, as an alterna-
tive to being scouted for bad spellers. Thus it
is that things originating in a weakness or per-
verse use of the reasoning faculties of an ancestor, may grow to be regarded as a virtue in a
descendant.

WH.

Our attention may now advert to the perfect
diagraph **WH**.

Alexander Gill, a contemporary of Shakespeare, and Head Master of St Paul's Schools,
wrote, "*W, aspiratum, consona est, quam scri-
bunt per* wh, *et tamen aspiratio præcedit.*" (W,
aspirated, is a consonant which is written *wh,*
and yet the Aspirate precedes it.) Dr Lowth
(1710-1787), Bishop of London, is quoted by

Mr Walker as having directed that WH should be pronounced " HW," this having been the relative positions of the letters during the Anglo-Saxon period. The erudite theory of the great Hebrew and Saxon scholar had a fascination for the theoretical orthoepist of whom Mr Cull, F.S.A., the learned editor of Ogilvie's Dictionary, writes :—

Mr Walker did not profess to record the current pronunciation of his day, but he sought to establish principles and even rules to govern the pronunciation ; and would change the pronunciation of words to bring them within his rules.

It is probable that Dr Lowth, who, practically, is the responsible author of this theory of inversion, was led to his conclusions as much by his belief that W was a vowel as by the historical considerations alluded to above. As regards W being always a vowel, Dr Lowth's argument was successfully refuted by Walker himself, whose statements in this respect, Posterity has endorsed. W is a vowel only when forming the latter half of a diphthong. And, moreover, even if the W were a vowel, Dr Lowth could have shewn no good reason for inverting the order of letters in pronouncing the digraph WH. The retrospective influence of a post-aspirate has no power to produce a breathing

on a vowel, or *on* a consonant ; but generally to
cause a vowel to *terminate* in a jerked breath
(*h'*) or a consonant to become unvocalised.
And again ; that Anglo-Saxon writers had been
wont to twist H round to the fore, was an
irrelevant fact, and one that ought to have had
no weight with the worthy bishop or with Mr
John Walker when engaged in dictating laws of
pronunciation to the English lieges of King
George III. When Walker wrote the following sentence concerning Dr Johnson, he was in
truth constructing a formula for his own
epitaph :—

His Dictionary has been deemed lawful plunder for
every subsequent lexicographer ; and so servilely has he
been copied, that his mistakes re-appear in several other
dictionaries.

And so it is that Mr Walker's second-hand
rule with regard to WH has retained the im-
plicit allegiance of all his successors who have
had pronouncing dictionaries to compile. In
the presence of such massive authority, to speak
is to be silenced, and to differ is to be crushed.
But still, as is seen in many things, the most
imposing and august array of venerable doctrine
cannot always stifle the "still small voice" of a
contrary conviction. Who shall say that Dr

Primrose had not been looking over a collection of pronouncing dictionaries, when he remarked that, as ten millions of circles can never make a square, so the united voice of myriads cannot lend the smallest foundation to the untrue.

A purpose of this treatise is to respectfully solicit of modern authorities a reconsideration of the doctrine of transposition or dictum relative to the WH ; and at the same time to lay certain data before the general reader.

Clear notions concerning the ordinary W are necessary to a proper appreciation of that variety occurring in WH.

The vowel-W is simply *oo ;* thus, in *pew,* "*ew*" is a diphthong and equal in sound to *ēoo.*

The consonant-W is a buzzed *oo* plus a rapid transition into the sound that succeeds it.   Let ⌇⌇⌇ represent the buzzed *oo,* and (the rapid transition :

$$W = (\text{⌇⌇⌇}( ).$$

If, while pronouncing *oo,* we narrow the labial aperture by approximating the edges of the upper and lower lips, the sound ⌇⌇⌇ is produced.   If, while producing the sound ⌇⌇⌇, we enlarge the labial aperture with sudden rapidity ((), a perfect consonant-W results.   Thus :

"we"=⌇⌇⌇(ē ; and, "woo"=⌇⌇⌇(oo.

Let WH be represented by ⋔.   The difference between W and ⋔ is that W is produced by vocalised breath and certain lip-movements

as described above ; whereas ⋏ is produced by
the *same lip-movements, but with unvocalised
breath.* Hence, in lieu of the buzzing sound, we
find in ⋏ a whispered or "whistled breath." It
is this breath-sound of ⋏ which has been so
persistently mistaken for the Aspirate H. The
sole office of the H in this digraph is to prescribe
the unvocalization of the W. The nature of the
subject renders it difficult to parade proofs of
these facts on the pages of a book, in order to
convince persons who, having a veneration for
Mr Walker's hoo hoo theory, might wish to up-
hold in theory that which they probably depart
from in practice. By careful attention to most
thoroughly good speakers it will be noticed that
an unvocalised W (⋏) is the phonic rendering
of the digraph WH; although the "whistled
breath" may be mistaken for an Aspirate by a
careless observer, or by one resolute in error.

It is not easy to understand why these facts
are not more widely recognised and insisted
upon by modern orthoepists and writers on
phonological science ; and it is very difficult
to attribute a cause to the longevity of the
erroneous notions that Mr Walker was an early
means of disseminating. When we see in our
pronouncing dictionaries that *whip* is to be pro-

nounced " hwip," the only belief open to us is that their writers intend two vowel-sounds to be heard in a word containing only one vowel ; for they can scarcely mean that the h shall aspirate a consonantal *w*, nor that a jerked *h'* shall precede‾ the word (thus *h'* + *wip*), nor can they desire that the h shall aspirate a whistle —HΛΛip. To say the least, the rendering of any of these would require a vocal gymnast to make it effective. But if two vowels *are* to be employed, the first must needs be aspirated and the second not ; so that a phonetic spelling of *whip* and *why* would be " hoo ip " and " hoo i "! And, according to Mr Walker and his disciples, this is the correct pronunciation. But the fact remains that even those gentlemen, who in their dictionaries have scrupulously reproduced Mr Walker's rule, have seldom been known to violate the principles of a correct pronunciation by adhering to it when speaking. The sore straits to which the rule occasionally reduces them might elicit pity. " Hw " is found to be unmanageable before *o* ; and therefore we find that since the days of Mr Walker, a perfect unanimity has prevailed among orthoepists with regard to the extrusion of W from the pronunciation of every word in which the digraph WH precedes an o; whence it comes that in all dictionaries in common use, *whole, whom, who*, &c., are phonetically expressed "hole," "hoom," "hoo," &c.; for, according to their method, to retain the W were to give these words the sound of hoo ole, hoo oom, and hoo oo! If, on the other hand, one remember that WH is an unvocalized W, no more hesitation will be experienced in giving it its due before an *o* than before any other vowel. ᴍole, ᴍoom, and ᴍoo, are quite as easy to pronounce as ᴍist, ᴍip, or ᴍale. *Who* is, however, very frequently made an exception by the best speakers of English, and pronounced "*hoo*." The word lost its ᴍ in the seventeenth century, and does not seem in a fair way to recover it.

Mr Ellis, so far as the writer is aware, is the only authority who has entered a protest against the modern conception of WH; and he gives it as his opinion that, from the earliest times, WH—whether mistaken for Hw or Hoo —has always been and still is, if rightly pronounced, WH.

This digraph is peculiar to the English language. English-speaking people differ in their manner of using it. In the south of England, it is seldom more than W; and *which* and *what* are pronounced " wich " and " wot." The educated classes must, by courtesy, be supposed without the pale of this accusation. In the northern parts of England WH is decidedly more correctly used ; in Scotland the pronunciation of it is perfect. In few cases would it be other than absurd to seek, out of England, for a criterion of English pronunciation ; but this is one of the exceptions wherein the norm is best found north of the Tweed. Scotch H's are harsh and grating, or like the H of HU (see page 37), or akin to the results of those guttural spasms that attend the primiparous aspirate-labours of a reformed H-dropper ; and the Scotch are known to wrongfully accuse Englishmen of dropping H's, that in reality have been properly aspirated ; but the Scotch neither exaggerate nor neglect the proper rendering of WH, and even their farm-labourers are worthy to be taken as models.* *Whale, whelp, when, where, whole,* are, in Scotland, dis-

---

* This only applies to occasions on which they indulge in *English* speech. The Anglo-Saxon WH (written *Hw*) had formerly a more palatal sound, and while passing into ʌʌ had a tendency to become *f.* In the Aberdeenshire dialect it has remained *f; e.g., fan, far =* when, where. Many such eccentric permutations are amusingly anaglyptographed in that monument of the "Aberdeenshire Doric," JOHNNY GIBB o' GUSHET-NEUK. (Ed'bro': D. Douglas.)

tinctly and properly, Male, Melp, Men, Mere, and Mole. Notwithstanding this indisputable fact, the four varieties of Ogilvie's excellent dictionary (the northern Scotchman's lexical fetish) give "hwale," "hwen," &c., as being the received pronunciation. In so doing they agree with all contemporary productions of their kind. The *rationale* of the inversion is a mystery; but a clue to the cause of this and other errors-upon-precedent, would very probably be found to have Mr John Walker at one end of it and the conservative spirit of subsequent orthoepists at the other.

PERMUTATION.

THE principles of reciprocal interchange of sounds, which are actively at work whenever new languages are coming into being, or old ones are splitting, or falling into decay, can only be adequately apprehended by obtaining a general but clear view of the entire scheme of philology. The annals of H would, however, be glaringly in default if no mention were made of its relations to foreign letters.

PHILOLOGY is a modern science. Leibnitz rescued it from the domain of pure fancy; Sir William Jones supplied it with ground to work upon; Bopp (a great authority on ancient Aspirates), Pott, and a host of others, began to build. The Greeks had been impressed with the idea that their language came from their gods; this made the study of alien tongues appear unimportant; hence, Greek philological research ended where it began. Analogous convictions shut the gates of progress on the most civilized of the Shemitic races. The Romans, again, when seeking to discover the origin of tongues, looked eastward for inspiration; but they did not look far enough. Long generations of their successors burrowed, like moles, in the Plains of Shinar. Grimm came, and there was light. The name of this great German philosopher has become so inseparably associated with the sudden strides made by modern linguistic science, as to have raised him from the ranks of philological pioneers, and placed him—in popular estimation—at the head and front of the whole enterprise. Whatever be the exact degree of his merit as a discoverer or thinker, as a successful propagator of rational views he stands a colossus and a marvel. Labled fragile by the sceptic, and dangerous by the orthodox, his theories out-lived both grimaces and frowns, and within a few years of their birth aroused Europe to the fact that a " Babel " had been, and still was, both within and around her ; and, seemingly by miracle, they even succeeded in carrying conviction and recognition of a truth that confuted tradition, to the very centres of some of the ecclesiastical circles of the day. Grimm's discoveries, while pointing out the slow but constant changes that languages undergo, showed also that all the languages of Europe and half those of Asia had sprung from a common origin— and that, not the Hebrew one dogmatically assigned to them by the Early Fathers. Fortunately for Grimm, he published in the beginning of the nineteenth century; had he been a contemporary of poor Galileo he might have been subjected to some inconvenience and censure.

Grimm — who, by-the-bye, was a bigoted patriot—devoted himself chiefly to an investigation of the Teutonic tongues, and to a study of the German language; but the result of his labours has shown the changes that sounds undergo when a word is being distributed among different peoples. The LAW bearing his name is tabulated below :—

Old Indo-European and Classic.	Introduced into Low German tongues (English, &c.)	In High German.
Aspirate sounds	become soft	hard
Soft „	„ hard	Aspirate
Hard „	„ Aspirate	soft

These rules are not without exceptions, but, especially in the case of sounds that begin words, the exceptions are not numerous enough to nullify the rule.

The following are some examples of permutation affecting the H :—

Sanskrit, Greek, and Latin hard sounds become Aspirate sounds in English ; example :—

$$\left.\begin{array}{ll} \textit{Sanskrit,} & \text{hrid } (=\textit{krid}) \\ \textit{Greek,} & \text{kardia} \\ \textit{Latin,} & \text{cor-dis} \end{array}\right\} = \begin{array}{l} \textit{English} \\ \textit{H}\text{eart.} \end{array}$$

The true English Aspirate corresponds to the Sanskrit K, and has nothing to do with the old Aryan *H*. The Latin H in *habere* has no Aryan root, and remains unexplained. English *have* is related to the Latin *capere*, not *habere*.

Sanskrit, Greek, and Latin Aspirates, represented by g :—

$$\left.\begin{array}{ll} \textit{Sanskrit,} & \text{Hansa} \\ \textit{Greek,} & \text{chen} \\ \textit{Latin,} & \text{(h)anser} \end{array}\right\} = \left\{\begin{array}{l} \textit{English,} \text{ goose.} \\ \textit{German,} \text{ gans.} \\ \textit{Russian,} \text{ gus.} \\ \textit{Breton,} \text{ gwaz.} \end{array}\right.$$

Some of the other changes that H undergoes in Indo-European languages may be briefly summarized :—

H = *ch*, example : Lat. *humus*, Gr. *chama*.

H = *chth* „ „ *hes, heri*, „ *chthes*.

H = *s* „ „ *septum*, „ *hepta*.

H = *w* „ „ many Greek words discarded the digamma for the Aspirate.

That H = *f*, has been shown in a Sabine and a Spanish example (page 24), and the same may be seen in a few French words—*e.g.*, Lat. *foris*, Fr. *hors;* and Lat. *fabulari*, Fr. *habler*. But the descendants of the Gauls are not chargeable with having reduced this last word to its present stunted condition ; the mutilation of *fabulari* was another act of vandalism perpetrated at an early date in Spain, the word having (according to Brachet*) crossed the Pyrenees, disguised as "*hablar*," in the sixteenth century.

* *Grammaire Historique* (1867). *Par* Auguste Brachet.

Disguises still more extraordinary happen in the Gothic languages. H is exchangeable with *c*. This substitution, together with the subsequent disappearance of the H, are causes of confusion, and often effectually conceal the relationship of cognate words. At first sight the English word *raw* seems to be considerably less than kin to the Italian *crudo;* but on collating the several synonymous words—English, *raw;* (Dutch, *raauw*); Saxon, *hreaw;* Latin, *cruor* and *crudus;* (French, *cru*), and Italian *crudo;* their family likeness and community of origin become a little more discernible.

The things of the Present are born of the Past, and are moulding the things of the Future ; the deeds of to-day show events of to-morrow reflected in shadowy outline. Conjectures concerning the future of H may be built on data afforded by its history. The Aspirate has grown enfeebled in Low-German tongues, and in Latin ones is almost discarded. It would bode evil to the continued existence of H, if either of these classes were to furnish the "universal language." But, probably one of them will. The *strong breathing* seems to be a remnant of that stage of transition which, at one time, may have formed a link between gesticulatory speech and the language of articulate sound. Then it was that every available accessory to the expression of the emotions will have been brought into use. And, *per contra*, in a highly developed state of

civilization, with its accompanying highly developed speech-code, the tones and modes of
expression that constituted nature's primitive
eloquence must fall gradually into disuse. The
strong breathing and the guttural breathing,
having been the most expressive emotional in-
terpreters of the early savage, are repugnant to
the artificial sedateness and studied reserve of
the modern speaker. In the speech of the well-
bred Englishman, the hale old English H has
melted into a soft Aspirate, and even this is
likely to be soon altogether lost. The French
say, " We regard aspirated H's with horror ! "—
Littré* declares they hurt his chest. Whatever
be the language spoken by Macaulay's New
Zealander, it is highly probable that he will drop
his H's.

• Another omen ⁓unfavourable to H is this.
Any letter doomed to die out of a word or a
language, generally attempts to depart grace-
fully by first acquiring the nature of an aspirate-
consonant, and then turns into a perfect H ;
under this form it relies upon h-dropping mortals
to give it quiet burial, and unobtrusively con-
fide it to Oblivion.

* " Je n'aime pas les H aspirées : cela fait mal à la
poitrine ; je suis pour l'euphonie."—VOLTAIRE.

F

APPENDIX.

[To the kindness of Professor Skeat of Cambridge
I am indebted for the following compend, wherein
the scientific grounds upon which a theoretical rule
for the silent H might be constructed, are perspicu-
ously exposed, while a practical view of the case is also
taken. A list of words with doubtful H's was submitted
to Professor Skeat, and the comments of this foremost
of British etymologists are a reply to the question :
What reasons can be found for the silencing of
the H's ?]

Of course the etymology has much to do
with it, so has accent, so has rapidity of speech,
so have individual notions.

(I.) ETYMOLOGY.

There are four principal H's — English,
French, Latin, and Greek.

As a *rule*, pronounce all but the French ; and,
of these, all but some words of Latin origin.

Examples. *English*—HILL, HOG, (though
this is properly Welsh), HUNT. The *h* should
never be omitted, being an original aspirate
of great strength.

French—herb, hospital, hostler, &c. By rule,

the *h* should be silent; but the word *herb*, in particular, has become so completely Anglicised that to hear an *h* in it is common. So also *habit, haughty, hearse, human; habit* and *human* being counted as Latin.

The H was sometimes omitted in the fourteenth century.

" As wrtis [wortis] of *erbis* soone thei shul falle doun."
Wycliffite version of Psalm xxxvii. 2, (earlier version).
" Thei schulen falle doun soone as the wortis of *eerbis.*"
Wycliffite version of Psalm xxxvii. 2, (later version).

But French words from Frankish, not Latin sources, take *h*, as *hamlet, halbert, harass, hatchet;* together with proper names, as *Henry, Hubert*. So also *harness*, a French word, but not of Latin origin.

Latin—The *h* is commonly sounded, as *horrid*. But *honorary* and *honorarium* follow the French word *honour*, and commonly omit *k*.

Greek—The *h* is important, as in *history*, *hexagon*, and should be sounded.

(2.) ACCENT.

Accent often drowns the *h*. Thus *history* takes *h*, but *historical* is usually *istorical*. To find this out, do not go by what people *say* they say (which is one thing), but by what you hear them say, which is a *very different matter*. Compare *hebdomadal, hallucination, hereditary, hiatus, histrionical, hippopotamus, hexameter, hieroglyphic, histology, horizon, hidalgo, homœopathy, horticulturist ;* in all these, the *h* is very weak.

(3) RAPIDITY.

Very common English words, as *have, here, has, him, her, his,* are pronounced '*ave,* '*ere,* in rapid speech. This will be denied stoutly by many who do so every day of their lives, especially in particular combinations. Much depends on the position of the word or the accent.

Ex. Did you see 'im go ?

Answer. I saw *him,* but not *her.*

It is *always* dropped, at the present day, in the old word *hem* (Chaucer), meaning *them. Ex.* I saw '*em* go.

(4.) INDIVIDUAL NOTIONS.

Particular people have particular opinions (frequently wrong ones) as to how words should be pronounced.

I think if you exercise your *ear* carefully, you will find it a better guide than written statements.